Inner and Outer Planets

by Kimberly Taylor

PEARSON
Scott
Foresman

What makes up the universe?

The Universe and the Milky Way

The **universe** includes all of space and everything in it. Most of the universe is empty space.

A **galaxy** is a system of gases, dust, and billions of stars clustered together. The universe has millions of galaxies. We live in the Milky Way galaxy. The Milky Way has a flat spiral shape. There are billions of stars in the Milky Way. The Sun is one of these stars. It is near the edge of our galaxy.

Astronomy is the study of the stars, the Sun, the Moon, and other objects in space. People have always been interested in objects in the sky. Experts think that the ancient Egyptians built the Great Pyramids to line up with the stars.

Other groups of people also studied astronomy long ago. Arabs, Chinese, Indians, Greeks, and others used astronomy to figure out the right time for planting or harvesting crops. Sailors used the Sun and the stars to find their way on the open sea.

Our Solar System

The **solar system** includes the planets, their moons, the Sun, and other objects. All objects in the solar system revolve around, or orbit, the Sun. A planet is a large, ball-shaped object that moves around a star such as the Sun. A planet is smaller and cooler than a star.

The planets closest to the Sun are Mercury, Venus, Earth, and Mars. They are the inner planets. The outer planets are Jupiter, Saturn, Uranus and Neptune. An area with many asteroids is between the inner and outer planets. Asteroids are rocky objects that are too small to be called planets.

The Sun's gravity keeps Earth and other space objects in their orbits. The orbits of the inner planets are shaped like circles. The orbits of the outer planets are more like ovals.

Asteroid belt

Jupiter

Earth

Sun

Venus

Mercury

Mars

The Sun

The Sun is the largest object in our solar system. It is a medium-sized star. The Sun is a huge ball of glowing, hot gases. The inner parts of the Sun are much hotter than the outer parts. Energy from the Sun gives heat and light to Earth.

The Sun has magnetism, just as Earth does. The magnetic field around some parts of the Sun can be very strong. Hot gas can burst from the surface of the Sun and form loops in these areas. Sunspots are dark spots on the Sun. They appear at very strong parts of the magnetic field.

The sizes and distances in this diagram are not true to scale. Also, the planets rarely line up.

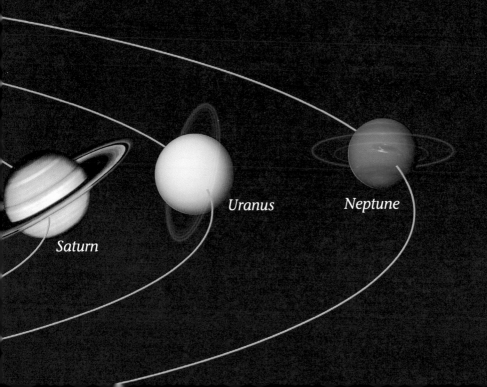

Saturn

Uranus

Neptune

What are the inner planets?

Mercury

Mercury is the planet closest to the Sun. It has thousands of dents called **craters.** They were formed by meteorites crashing into Mercury's surface. A meteorite is a rock from space that hits a planet.

A **space probe** is a vehicle that uses cameras and other tools to study different objects in space. In 1974 the *Mariner 10* space probe was sent to Mercury.

Too Hot and Too Cold

There is almost no atmosphere on Mercury. It is very hot during the day. Without an atmosphere to hold heat, Mercury is very cold at night.

Mercury Facts

Average distance from Sun
57,900,000 km (35,983,000 mi)

Diameter
4,879 km (3,032 mi)

Length of day as measured in Earth time
59 days

Length of year as measured in Earth time
88 days

Average surface temperature
117°C (332°F)

Moons
none

Weight of a person who is 100 lb on Earth
38 lb

Venus

Venus is about the same size as Earth. It is the second planet from the Sun. Venus is very dry and hot, just as Mercury is. However, Venus has an atmosphere. This atmosphere is made of thick, swirling clouds. These clouds are very hot and poisonous. Venus has strong winds and a lot of lightning. Its clouds reflect sunlight well. At night Venus is one of the brightest objects we see in the sky.

Venus Facts

Average distance from Sun
108,200,000 km (67,200,000 mi)

Diameter
12,104 km (7,521 mi)

Length of day as measured in Earth time
243 days (spins backward)

Length of year as measured in Earth time
225 days

Average surface temperature
464°C (867°F)

Moons
none

Weight of a person who is 100 lb on Earth
91 lb

Earth

Earth is the largest rocky planet in the solar system. It is the third planet from the Sun. It is the only planet whose surface has liquid water. In fact, water covers most of its surface.

Earth is surrounded by a layer of gas called the atmosphere. The atmosphere makes life possible. It keeps some of the Sun's harmful rays from reaching Earth. The atmosphere is mostly nitrogen, water vapor, carbon dioxide, and oxygen. Animals and plants use these gases. Earth is the only planet in the solar system known to have life on it.

Earth Facts

Average distance from Sun
149,600,000 km (93,000,000 mi)

Diameter
12,756 km (7,926 mi)

Length of day as measured in Earth time
24 hours

Length of year as measured in Earth time
365 days

Average surface temperature
15°C (59°F)

Moons
1

Weight of a person who is 100 lb on Earth
100 lb

The Moon

A **satellite** is an object that orbits another object in space. Moons are satellites of planets. They revolve around planets just as planets revolve around the Sun. A moon stays in orbit around a planet because of the force of gravity between the moon and the planet.

Earth has one moon. Earth is about fifty times the size of its moon. The Moon has no atmosphere. It has many craters caused by meteorites.

Exploring the Moon

Sputnik was the first artificial satellite. It was launched in 1957 by the former Soviet Union. In 1959, the Soviet Union sent the first probes to the Moon. No people were on these probes.

The first person to travel in space was Russian cosmonaut Yuri Gagarin. In 1961, he circled Earth in less than two hours in the spaceship *Vostok I*. The first people to step on the Moon were Americans Neil Armstrong and Buzz Aldrin in 1969. Their footprints will stay there for years because the Moon has no wind or rain to wash them away.

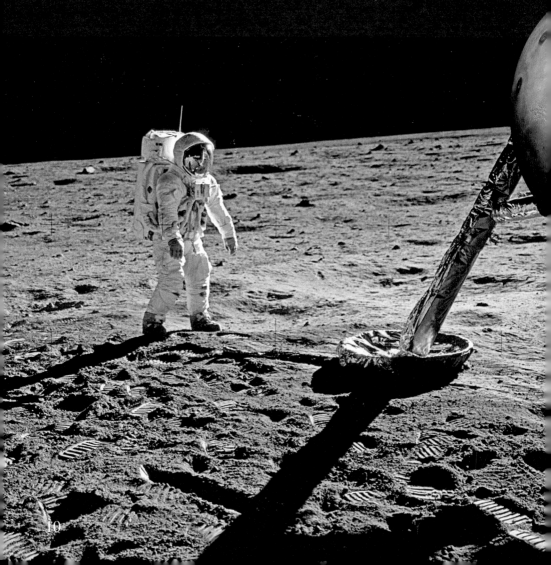

Mars is the fourth planet from the Sun. It is covered by rocks and soil that are made of the mineral iron oxide. Iron oxide is reddish brown. Because of this, Mars is nicknamed the "Red Planet." Mars has two moons with deep craters. Phobos, one of its moons, is very close to Mars.

Winds on Mars cause dust storms that are large enough to cover the entire planet. There is not enough oxygen in the atmosphere of Mars to support life forms such as plants and animals.

Mars has volcanoes and a canyon that is bigger than Earth's Grand Canyon. Mars also has polar ice caps.

Several probes have landed on Mars. They have sent data back to Earth.

Mars Facts

Average distance from Sun
227,900,000 km (141,600,000 mi)

Diameter
6,794 km (4,222 mi)

Length of day as measured in Earth time
24.6 hours

Length of year as measured in Earth time
687 days

Average surface temperature
−63°C (−81°F)

Moons
2

Weight of a person who is 100 lb on Earth
38 lb

What do we know about Jupiter, Saturn, and Uranus?

Jupiter

Jupiter is the fifth planet from the Sun. It is the largest planet in the solar system. Jupiter is so big that all of the other planets would fit inside of it! Jupiter is a gas giant. A gas giant is a very large planet made mostly of gases. Most of Jupiter's atmosphere is hydrogen and helium. Jupiter has rings. They are too dark to be seen from Earth.

The Great Red Spot is a weather system in Jupiter's atmosphere. It has been active for centuries. It is more than three times the size of Earth.

Jupiter Facts

Average distance from Sun
778,400,000 km (484,000,000 mi)

Diameter
142,984 km (88,846 mi)

Length of day as measured in Earth time
10 hours

Length of year as measured in Earth time
12 years

Average surface temperature
−148°C (−234°F)

Moons
at least 63

Rings
yes

Weight of a person who is 100 lb on Earth
214 lb

Jupiter's Moons

At least 63 moons orbit Jupiter. The four largest moons are about the same size as Earth's moon. The names of the four largest moons are Io, Europa, Ganymede, and Callisto. Io has the most active volcanoes of any body in the solar system. Europa has a frozen crust that may have a liquid ocean underneath. Ganymede is the largest moon in the solar system. It is bigger than Pluto and Mercury! Callisto has more craters than any other object in the solar system.

Io

Europa

Ganymede

Callisto

Saturn is also a gas giant. It is the sixth planet from the Sun. Helium and hydrogen make up most of its atmosphere. Saturn is huge, but it has only a small amount of solid matter.

The space probe *Voyager* explored the rings around Saturn. It found that the particles that make up the rings are many different sizes. Some are as small as grains of sand. Others are as large as boulders. The particles are probably made of rock, dust, and ice.

Moons of Saturn

Pan   Atlas   Prometheus   Janus

Mimas

Pandora

Epimetheus

Enceladus

Saturn Facts

Average distance from Sun
1,426,725,000 km (885,900,000 mi)

Diameter
120,536 km (74,897 mi)

Length of day as measured in Earth time
11 hours

Length of year as measured in Earth time
29.4 years

Average surface temperature
−178°C (−288°F)

Moons
at least 34

Rings
yes

Weight of a person who is 100 lb on Earth 74 lb

Galileo's Handles

Galileo thought he was seeing a planet with handles when he saw Saturn through his telescope. The handles were actually the rings around the planet.

Moons of Saturn

Saturn has at least 34 moons. Most of Saturn's moons are small. Titan is its largest moon. It has an atmosphere. It is larger than both Mercury and Pluto.

Tethys

Dione

Rhea

Titan

Hyperion

Iapetus

Phoebe

Uranus is the seventh planet from the Sun. It is the farthest planet you can see without a telescope. William Herschel discovered it in 1781. Uranus is a gas giant. It has an atmosphere of hydrogen, helium, and methane. Tiny drops of methane make a thin cloud that covers the planet. This gives Uranus its fuzzy, blue–green appearance. The temperature on Uranus is very cold.

Uranus has a ring system and many moons. The rings are dark and hard to see from Earth.

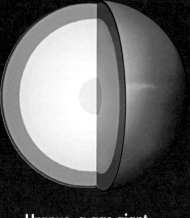

Uranus, a gas giant, has a large, liquid core.

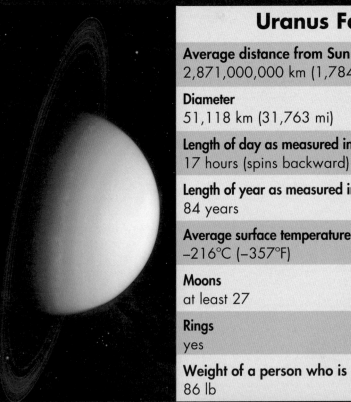

Uranus Facts

Average distance from Sun
2,871,000,000 km (1,784,000,000 mi)

Diameter
51,118 km (31,763 mi)

Length of day as measured in Earth time
17 hours (spins backward)

Length of year as measured in Earth time
84 years

Average surface temperature
–216°C (–357°F)

Moons
at least 27

Rings
yes

Weight of a person who is 100 lb on Earth
86 lb

Rolling Through Space

Uranus spins on its side. No one is sure why it is tilted this way. Scientists think that a very large object may have hit Uranus when the solar system was forming. This bump may have knocked the planet on its side.

The Moons of Uranus

Uranus has at least 27 moons. The moons closer to the planet were first seen through telescopes during the 1700s. They are large moons with steep ridges, craters, and deep valleys. The moons farthest from Uranus are hard to see from Earth, even with telescopes.

Ariel

Titania

Oberon

Miranda

Umbriel

What do we know about Neptune and beyond?

Neptune

Neptune is the smallest of the gas giants. It is the eighth planet from the Sun. Neptune is too far away to be seen without a telescope. Astronomers discovered Neptune in 1846.

Neptune has a very long orbit because it is so far from the Sun. One trip around the Sun takes Neptune 165 Earth years. Strong winds blow huge storms such as the Great Dark Spot across the planet.

Methane gas gives Neptune a blue color. It has bands of clouds and storms.

Neptune Facts

Average distance from Sun
4,498,300,000 km (2,795,000,000 mi)

Diameter
49,528 km (30,775 mi)

Length of day as measured in Earth time
16 hours

Length of year as measured in Earth time
165 years

Average surface temperature
−214°C (−353°F)

Moons
at least 13

Rings
yes

Weight of a person who is 100 lb on Earth
110 lb

How Neptune Was Discovered

Astronomer John Couch Adams studied objects in space, including planets. He noticed that Uranus wasn't orbiting the way he thought it should be. He felt that the odd orbit was caused by gravity of another planet. A mathematician named Urbain Leverrier also studied this idea. He predicted the position and size of the other planet. On September 23, 1846, Johann Galle pointed his telescope where the predictions said he should look. He saw Neptune!

The Moons of Neptune

Neptune's largest moon is Triton. It has a surface temperature of about −235°C. Astronomers think that Triton formed farther from the Sun than Neptune did. They think it was captured by Neptune's gravity.

Triton

Neptune's ring

Neptune

Pluto

Clyde Tombaugh discovered Pluto in 1930. Until 2006, Pluto was called a planet. Now scientists call Pluto a dwarf planet. A dwarf planet is a small, ball-shaped object that orbits around the Sun. Pluto is smaller than the Earth's moon!

Pluto has a moon named Charon. It is a little smaller than Pluto. The planets that have moons are much larger than their moons. Pluto has at least two other moons.

Pluto orbits past Neptune. Sometimes it is closer to the Sun than Neptune. The outer planets are gas giants. Pluto is not a gas giant. It has a solid, icy surface.

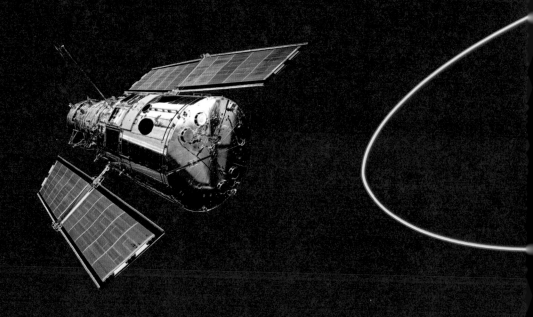

An Odd Orbit

Pluto travels around the Sun at a different angle than the planets do. Pluto has a tilted orbit. During part of its orbit, Pluto is closer to the Sun than Neptune is. This happened from 1979 to 1999. The next time this will happen is in 2237.

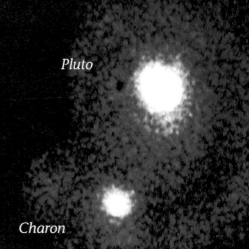

Pluto

Charon

In 2003, scientists found a dwarf planet that is a little larger than Pluto. It orbits at least three times farther from the Sun than Pluto. It has at least one moon. This dwarf planet was called 2003 UB313, but in 2006 it was named Eris.

Scientists have seen other things that are even farther out in the solar system than Pluto and Eris. But these things are probably too small to be planets or dwarf planets.

Our solar system is only a tiny part of the gigantic universe. Earth is only a small part of the solar system. Mercury, Venus, Earth, and Mars are the four planets closest to the Sun. These inner planets are small and rocky. Jupiter, Saturn, Uranus, and Neptune are outer planets. They are gas giants with many moons. Neptune and Pluto are too far from the Sun to be seen without a powerful telescope. Astronomers have seen other objects beyond Pluto, but these objects seem too small to be planets.

Glossary

astronomy   the study of the Sun, the Moon, stars, and other objects in space

craters   bowl-shaped dents on the surface of planets

galaxy   a system of gases, dust, and billions of stars clustered together

satellite   an object that orbits another object in space

solar system   the Sun, the planets, their moons, and other objects that revolve around the Sun

space probe   a vehicle that carries cameras and other tools to study objects in space

universe   all of space and everything in it

What did you learn?

1. What are some differences between inner and outer planets?

2. How were Mercury's craters made?

3. Why will astronauts' footprints remain on the Moon's surface for years?

4. **Writing** in Science Neptune was discovered in 1846. On your own paper, describe how scientists discovered this planet. Include details from the book to support your answer.

5. **Predict** Do you think more moons of Jupiter will be discovered? Why or why not?

Genre	Comprehension Skill	Text Features	Science Content
Nonfiction	Predict	• Captions • Call Outs • Text Boxes • Glossary	Solar System

Scott Foresman Science 4.18

ISBN-13: 978-0-328-34241-9
ISBN-10:   0-328-34241-6

scottforesman.com

Space and Technology

The Sun
and the Seasons

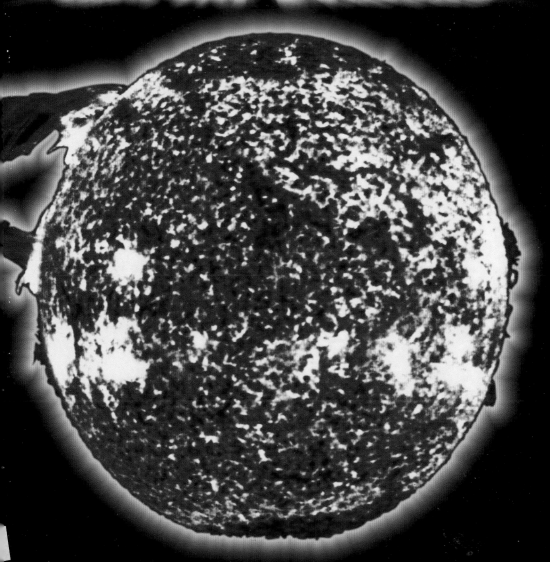

by Peggy Bresnick Kendler

Vocabulary

axis
constellation
lunar eclipse
phase
revolution
rotation
star
telescope

Extended Vocabulary

ellipse
equator
equinox
gravitational pull
hemisphere
orbit
solstice

Picture Credits

Every effort has been made to secure permission and provide appropriate credit for photographic material.
The publisher deeply regrets any omission and pledges to correct errors called to its attention in subsequent editions.

Photo locators denoted as follows: Top (T), Center (C), Bottom (B), Left (L), Right (R), Background (Bkgd).

2 Getty Images; 3 Getty Images; 9 (CR)Georg Gerster/Photo Researchers, Inc.; 12 (B)Nigel Hicks/Alamy Images;
13 (TR)Bruce Adams/Eye Ubiquitous; 15 Stephane Masson /Corbis; 16 (TR)Getty Images; 20 SYGMA/Corbis.

Scott Foresman/Dorling Kindersley would also like to thank: 7 NASA/DK Images; 14 NASA/DK Images.

Unless otherwise acknowledged, all photographs are the copyright © of Dorling Kindersley, a division of Pearson.